T0034589

"It has been so refreshing to read such a clear explanation of the different aspects that make up the dyslexia concept. This is a gift to parents and schools who need a professional but easy-to-digest understanding of dyslexia. This understanding is then put into a living context, by the hilarious, imaginative and emotionally intuitive story about a child surmounting the barriers that dyslexia-type difficulties can cause."

Caro Strover,
Educational Psychologist

A Nasty Dose of the Yawns

Zack has always found school difficult. Even though he is good at maths and excellent at flicking elastic bands, trying to read and write is like trying to fight a kraken. One day, when he discovers the rest of his class infected by a mysterious sleeping sickness, Zack draws on his strengths resulting in some unexpected consequences . . .

This engaging story, suitable for readers aged 8–12, explores some of the challenges faced by learners who find literacy unusually difficult. Alongside the practical difficulties of living in a world that assumes good levels of literacy, it explores some of the psychological impacts of struggling to achieve a skill that most children acquire with relative ease. Ultimately, it shows children that they can draw on their strengths and overcome the challenges in their way.

Also available as a set with a supporting guide, this book operates as a fun and entertaining standalone story, as well as an educational opportunity. The range of vocabulary means it can be used flexibly, for independent, paired or whole-group reading. It is a must-have book for every classroom.

Plum Hutton is a chartered educational psychologist and former learning support teacher. She holds a doctorate in educational psychology. She has more than 15 years of experience working as a local authority educational psychologist and latterly has transferred to independent practice. Through her work she has pursued and delivered training on many areas of professional interest, including supporting children with persistent anxiety, attachment difficulties, literacy difficulties and sensory processing differences.

Plum is a keen storyteller. She has gathered inspiration for her writing from her work, the challenges of parenthood and also through a nomadic existence as an Army wife, which has taken her to many locations across the UK and as far afield as East Africa.

Adventures with Diversity

**An Adventure with Autism and Social Communication Difficulties:
The Man-Eating Sofa Storybook and Guidebook**
The Man-Eating Sofa: An Adventure with
Autism and Social Communication Difficulties
Supporting Autism and Social Communication
Difficulties in Mainstream Schools:
A Guidebook for *The Man-Eating Sofa*

**An Adventure with Dyslexia and Literacy Difficulties:
A Nasty Dose of the Yawns Storybook and Guidebook**
A Nasty Dose of the Yawns: An Adventure with
Dyslexia and Literacy Difficulties
Supporting Dyslexia and Literacy Difficulties in Schools:
A Guidebook for *A Nasty Dose of the Yawns*

**An Adventure with Childhood Obesity:
Down Mount Kenya on a Tea Tray Storybook and Guidebook**
Down Mount Kenya on a Tea Tray: An Adventure with
Childhood Obesity
Supporting Childhood Obesity in Schools:
A Guidebook for *Down Mount Kenya on a Tea Tray*

A Nasty Dose of the Yawns

An Adventure with Dyslexia and Literacy Difficulties

Plum Hutton

Illustrated by Freddie Hodge

Routledge
Taylor & Francis Group

LONDON AND NEW YORK

Cover image: Freddie Hodge

First published 2022
by Routledge
2 Park Square, Milton Park, Abingdon, Oxon OX14 4RN

and by Routledge
605 Third Avenue, New York, NY 10158

Routledge is an imprint of the Taylor & Francis Group, an informa business

British Library Cataloguing-in-Publication Data
A catalogue record for this book is available from the British Library

Library of Congress Cataloging-in-Publication Data
A catalog record has been requested for this book

ISBN: 978-1-032-07640-9 (pbk)
ISBN: 978-1-003-20808-2 (ebk)

DOI: 10.4324/9781003208082

Typeset in Helvetica
by Deanta Global Publishing Services, Chennai, India

To Dowie and Dakbar and the wonderful dynasty
that they created and nurtured

———

Contents

Acknowledgements

I would like to extend my thanks to:

Iona and Ramsay Hutton for their encouragement and youthful perspective

Claire Anson, Karin Twiss, Fran Townend and Emma Judge for their support and advice

Alex Hutton for his patience, optimism and support during the writing of this book.

Prologue

The ofsted wriggled and stretched so that his long claws scraped the top of his nest. He slumped on to his tummy, eyelids fluttering through a dream-soaked sleep. In his mind he was young again, scampering through meadows in the evening sun with a rabble of ofsteds weaving between the trees, chasing, tumbling and chattering with mischief. He could smell fresh grass and damp moss, and hear the sounds of friendship.

His rasping snoring woke him from his slumber, and he lay sodden with sleep trying to organise his mind. Slowly he became aware of his senses and recognised the familiar feelings of stiff, cold bones and his eyes blinded by the darkness – but, worst of all, an aching loneliness. He was old and alone, with nothing to look forward to except the dreams of his youth. Or so he thought . . .

DOI: 10.4324/9781003208082-1

Chapter One

The slug oozed between Ben's fingers and flopped on to the back of his hand. Ned and Ben were huddled at the back of the line, as Year 6 waited to enter Applehurst Primary School. There was nothing unusual about the day; the sun shone cheerfully through the trees and a warm breeze skittered around the playground. Ben was annoyed at having to put the ginger monster back in Ned's pocket. Here it joined other slugs to make a creeping ball of slime.

Ned was very proud of his slug collection. He had six different types and they all had names like 'stink' and 'snot'. He rarely brought them into school, because his mother always complained about his pockets being stuck together when she came to wash his trousers. Also, the slugs didn't like living in Ned's pocket. They kept trying to squeeze out through a hole in his trousers. Ned worried that one might get lost.

Ben grinned at the thick slick of orange slime that was now stuck to the back of his hand. "That's so cool!" he whispered. "We must show Zack at lunchtime."

"Yeah, Ginger Gunge is the best slimer of all," replied Ned, "and he moves really fast. I can feel him crawling down my leg already."

"Cooooool!" repeated Ben.

DOI: 10.4324/9781003208082-2

The headteacher, Miss Bertha Crimpet, wrinkled her nose as she watched the children file in from the playground. She wasn't feeling her best after a rather late night with Dr Bling, the new doctor from the health centre next to the school. She slurped the last of her coffee and sighed, glancing in the small mirror on the wall beside her. She hoped to see a keen, attractive, intelligent woman staring back, but her reflection seemed grey and droopy this morning, so she reached for another cup of coffee. At least it would be a quiet day with Years 4 and 5 out on a trip.

Standing at the classroom door, Miss Hazel was ready to greet each of her pupils in turn and tick them off on the register as they passed. She tried to keep her mind on the job, but her whole body was tingling with excitement and joy. She was IN LOVE! She felt that any moment she would throw the register to the ground and run off around the playground, with her arms flung wide, singing about the beauty of the day and the love in her heart. She was getting MARRIED! Life was good. But, on reflection, she would still need a job after her honeymoon, so perhaps running around the playground like a wailing lunatic was not the best idea. At least it was Creative Arts Week, and she had planned some really messy art projects, which would be a welcome break from spelling and multiplication.

Miss Hazel drew in a deep breath and focused on the line of waiting children. Bella was first in line as always, looking too perfect and too keen to be popular with the rest of the class.

"Good morning, Bella."

"Morning, Miss Hazel."

"Top marks again for your English extension work. Well done." Bella blazed with smug pride.

"Good morning, Amy. Has your tortoise turned up?"

"No, Miss Hazel. He's been gone for a week. My dad thinks he's run off to find a lady tortoise, but I don't know of any lady tortoises near us, so he's probably lonely."

"I'm sorry to hear that," said Miss Hazel, with genuine concern. "Perhaps he's enjoying an adventure in the wild for a bit. I'll keep my fingers crossed that he turns up again soon. Good morning, Emily." And so she continued until she reached Ben and Ned, at the end of the line as always.

"Good morning, Ben."

"Morning, Miss Hazel."

"We need to have another look at the sums you did last lesson. Some of them have gone a bit wonky."

"Uh, OK," replied Ben, trying to clean the slime off his hand by wiping it repeatedly on the seat of his trousers.

"Good morning, Ned," said Miss Hazel brightly, fixing him with a penetrating stare. "There appears to be something odd going on in your pocket," she remarked, looking down at the pair of tentacles feeling their way out of Ned's pocket. "Do I need to know about it?"

"Erm. No, Miss Hazel. Nothing you need to worry about." She raised an eyebrow.

"Good, I thought so," she replied, deciding not to take action on this occasion. She made a mental note to keep a close eye on Ned this morning, even closer than usual.

Glancing down at her register, Miss Hazel noted that Zack Snodgrass was missing. She frowned; it was unlike him to be late, even though school was tough for him.

A sudden image flashed through her brain: a vivid memory of Zack on the first day they had properly met. It was when she had been teaching Year 3. She had noticed him at the back of the class, a furious expression fixed on his face beneath his dark, chaotic hair. Unaware that he was being observed, he slumped over his desk, pulled a clump of elastic bands from his pocket and began firing them, one by one, at the display boards that ran along the edge of the room. Miss Hazel finished her conversation with another pupil and waited until Zack had run out of ammunition. He lay with his cheek on the desk flicking his pencil up and down, up and down with his index finger. She knew about Zack and his difficulties. His reputation for tricky behaviour had preceded him.

Zack suddenly looked up, catching her eye defiantly, and then returned his cheek to the desk.

Miss Hazel slid open the drawer of her desk and drew out a handful of elastic bands. She crossed the classroom and nimbly squatted down in front of Zack's desk so that their eyes met across the table. She was aware of other children following her actions but she ignored them. Zack was tensed, waiting for the inevitable reprimand, braced for the usual comments about his disappointing behaviour and lack of work. She could see his mind working out which response he would use on this occasion – perhaps sullenly ignoring her, or shouting insults, or throwing his chair to the ground and storming out into the playground. That last option was probably his favourite. She had often seen him angrily pacing around outside, shoulders hunched and hands thrust deep in his pockets, a thundercloud of fury following in his wake. *This time is going to be different*, thought Miss Hazel.

"I bet you can't hit the middle of the clock," she challenged, pushing her handful of elastic bands towards his nose. Zack's eyebrows sprang up to his hairline in surprise. He glanced at the elastic bands suspiciously, anticipating a trick. She pushed them a little closer.

"Go on. You've got three shots," she said quietly, gesturing towards the large, round clock in the centre of the wall.

The whole class was listening now, staring in silent anticipation of a disaster. Zack glanced back at Miss Hazel and then slowly reached down, selected an elastic band from the pile and very deliberately aimed it at the clock. It shot from his fingers with a satisfying twang and slapped into the number 8 on the clock face. Miss Hazel nodded.

"Not bad for a first attempt, but the middle would be better."

Zack glared at her and swiftly reached for another elastic band. Deftly, he stretched it between his fingers and *Twang!* it shot across the room, landing smack in the centre of the clock. Zack beamed at Miss Hazel, his eyes gleaming with defiant triumph.

"Good," she said calmly. "Was that a fluke or can you do it again?" Zack straightened his back, ready for the challenge.

"Go on, Zack, you can do it!" encouraged Ned.

"Yeah. Right in the middle," shouted Ben from across the classroom.

Miss Hazel glanced around her and the children fell silent again, all eyes trained on the clock. Zack was mindful of his audience, and he delicately grasped a thick red elastic band between thumb and index finger. He took aim and *Pow!* straight into the centre of the clock.

"Yessss!" A collective roar of triumph rolled around the class. Zack punched the air, grinning with a proper smile that crinkled his eyes. He absorbed the praise of his classmates like a parched plant, greedily soaking up water.

Miss Hazel waited for the hubbub to die down before turning to address the class. "Tomorrow we shall make a target on the wall and we can have an elastic band flicking challenge before lunch. I suspect Zack will be the one to beat."

"Yay!" cried the class, chattering to their neighbours and planning tactics. Miss Hazel again crouched down and studied Zack.

"Well, we've already found one thing that you're good at. That's not a bad start," she smiled. "Now can you gather up your ammunition, please?" She gestured to the scattering of elastic bands lying on the floor. Zack clambered out of his chair, still grinning. Meanwhile, Miss Hazel took his book, where he should have been writing a few lines about himself and what he enjoyed doing. She wrote in large deliberate writing, on alternate lines. When he returned to his seat, she pointed to the words on the page.

"Have a go at copying these sentences, please. Let's read them together."

"My name is Zack. I am amazing at firing elastic bands at a target. I have just started Year 3 and it is going to be great!" Zack smiled and nodded.

"Come and see me at lunchtime. We are going to make a plan together about your reading and writing. OK?" Zack nodded again, holding her gaze for a while, before setting to work painstakingly copying out the letters, his tongue sticking out of the side of his mouth in concentration.

It had been at lunchtime on that first day in Year 3 that she had sat alone with Zack and listened. She listened as Zack's frustration poured out. She felt his anger at not being able to read the same books as his friends. She absorbed his feelings of despair when he had good ideas but was unable to write them down. She noted his bitterness at the way the less tactful members of the class implied that he was stupid because his handwriting was a mess. They sniggered at his spelling mistakes, and yet he knew that he could calculate most maths sums faster than anyone else in his year. He never teased them about being rubbish at maths. Miss Hazel listened, as Zack explained how his mother blamed herself for his problems and how he blamed himself for his mother's anxieties. She heard how he missed his dad, who often worked away from home and was not around much to help. She saw the fatigue of repeated failure in the droop of his shoulders.

She allowed the wave of emotions to wash around the classroom for a few moments and for Zack's breathing to slow again before she replied.

"Zack, I've seen already that you have many strengths. Your verbal skills in lessons are excellent. You're friendly and helpful and you're popular with the rest of the class, and you are right, your maths skills are really strong for your age." Zack looked at his feet, as though he found it hard to believe this praise.

"What's more, I would put money on you winning the elastic band flicking competition tomorrow." At this, he looked up and grinned.

"It was a good shot, wasn't it?"

"An excellent shot," agreed Miss Hazel, smiling with him before becoming serious again.

"Zack, has anyone talked to you about dyslexia?"

"Yeah. My mum said that Miss Crimpet had mentioned it."

"We need to keep monitoring you for a bit before we can be sure, but I think it is likely that you are dyslexic."

"Does it mean that I'm thick?"

"No, not at all. It is a common problem, and it doesn't mean that you are unintelligent, just that you find reading and writing more difficult than most other people. With some support, I am optimistic that we can overcome this problem." She paused for breath and then ploughed on. "The first thing we are going to check is that your ears and eyes are working properly. Then I'm going to find out what you already know and start from there. I am confident that you can learn to read."

Zack looked doubtful. "I've not managed to do it so far," he pointed out.

"Well, you've already learnt the basics, so I'm sure you can learn more," she said firmly. "I'm going to arrange for you to read every day with either me or Mrs Conway. The more you practise, the easier it should become."

Zack still looked uncertain, so Miss Hazel continued.

"I know you find this difficult and have been struggling with it for several years, but if you can try to think positively, you will be more likely to succeed." She paused, thinking for a moment. "When I am finding something difficult, I find it helpful to have a phrase I can say to myself to give me courage."

"Like what?"

"My phrase is: *I can do this; I'm a strong and independent woman.*"

"No offence, Miss, but that's not going to work for me. I don't really want to be a woman."

"Well, of course it won't work for you. That's **my** phrase; we need to think of one for you."

"Oh." Zack thought for a bit. "Well, everything feels like a battle, so how about something to do with conquering?"

"Good idea," she replied, "and in your heart of hearts, do you think you are stupid?"

"No, I think I'm smart. I'm just not good at reading."

"I agree. So how about a phrase like *I'm smart; I can conquer this*," she suggested. Zack thought for a bit.

"It's not a very exciting phrase."

"No," agreed Miss Hazel, "but it says the right thing. You can think up some better ones over the weekend. Now, one more thing before you go for lunch. I think we ought to give this problem a name. This might sound crazy, but it can help to imagine the reading and writing difficulties as being like a monster that we can all work together to conquer. It allows us to think of the problem as being separate from you, rather than feeling that **you** are the problem. So we can talk about the monster causing problems today or trying some new strategies to squash the monster."

"Hmm." Zack liked this idea. He could get angry with the monster, rather than feeling angry with himself all the time.

"What do you think your reading and writing monster might look like? It's totally up to you. It depends on your imagination."

"A kraken," replied Zack without hesitation.

"A kraken?" said Miss Hazel "You'll have to remind me. What is a kraken?"

"It's like a giant squid. It lurks in the bottom of the sea and then emerges from the depths to grab sailing boats" – Zack illustrated his point by waving his arms in the air like a furious octopus – "and then it drags them beneath the waves to their deaths."

"Oh my. It sounds terrifying."

"Ooh, it is," agreed Zack with gleaming eyes, before frowning and chewing his lip. "I suppose my reading difficulties are like a kraken. Every time I relax, they seem to reach out and pull me down."

"Well, this year, we are going to make The Kraken less problematic. I'm going to teach you strategies that you can use to squish The Kraken, to reduce its power, to allow you to sail in whatever direction the wind takes you."

"I'm smart; I can conquer The Kraken," declared Zack, proudly puffing out his chest.

"You certainly can!" Miss Hazel replied.

Miss Hazel blinked the memory away, staring down once again at the register. That had been three years ago, and she was now teaching him again, as Miss Crimpet had asked her to teach Year 6 this year. She was determined to make it another good year for him. *Where was Zack?* she pondered. Then she remembered. He was having another hearing test at the hospital and would be back after lunch.

Blast! she thought. *Of all the mornings for him not to be in school when they would be doing no literacy work at all.* He had made huge progress and was top of the class in maths and science, but writing remained torturous for him. A strand of her long dark hair strayed across her nose, and she tucked it behind her ear in a well-practised movement. Well, it couldn't be helped. He could join in this afternoon. She snapped shut her register and slipped into the classroom. Today was going to be AWESOME!

Chapter Two

Miss Hazel kept her good mood during circle time, despite having to explain that the elderly class hamster had escaped and eaten a jumbo-sized glue stick.

"It is a shame that Nibbles was so greedy," she said. "Hamsters don't eat glue in the wild and I am afraid that he died in the night." There was a murmur of distress but the class took the news surprisingly calmly and decided that a short funeral at the end of the day would be a good idea. Ned saw a big ginger tentacle waving out of his pocket and gently pushed it back down to the bottom to join the other slugs. Little did he know that in a few hours his slugs would be involved in a major medical disaster.

Soon the fun began. Miss Hazel asked the class to make a huge model of the Spanish Armada being burnt by English fireships off the coast of England. They set to work making Spanish ships, English ships, fire, sea and the white cliffs of Dover. Ned and Ben began making lots of little Spanish sailors, who all seemed to be dying in nasty ways.

Bella worked away, intent on creating a perfect fireship. The English had cleverly sailed several flaming ships into the Spanish fleet, causing many of them to catch fire and sink. Bella critically studied her handiwork. The fireship

 DOI: 10.4324/9781003208082-3

was not quite bright enough for her liking, and she was determined that her creation would be flawless. She explained her problem to Miss Hazel and asked permission to look in the very back of the art cupboard to find some really vibrant tissue paper. Few people explored the back of the art cupboard, which was dark and slightly smelly. It had become a dumping ground for half-finished exercise books, cardboard, blunt scissors and empty washing-up liquid bottles. However, there were some long-forgotten treasures, such as a wonderful selection of tissue paper. What no one knew was that an old and mangy ofsted was living in the tissue paper.

Most people have never heard of ofsteds, as they are usually only found in forests in Eastern Europe. This one had accidentally arrived a few years ago with a Polish family. It had made a comfortable home in the tissue paper in Miss Hazel's art cupboard. Here it had stayed, only coming out at night to eat drops of chocolate spread and shards of crisps left over from the children's packed lunches. The ofsted had once been a cheery soul, but he was old, tatty and lonely now, and he missed the forests of his homeland. He was always sleepy and befuddled. His fur itched with strange yellow dust. He hated being disturbed.

The ofsted blinked and hunched deeper into the tissue as Bella carried the large mound of paper to Miss Hazel's desk. A huddle of children soon gathered around, all keen to grab the best colours for their projects. The ofsted was terrified. He remained perfectly still, curled out of sight as pieces of tissue were whipped from under him. Bella had unearthed a stunning range of rainbow colours, and as the first children began returning to their desks with sheets of scarlet, sizzling orange and deep purple, there was a second rush of children eager to find the colour of their choice. A crowd of seven or eight children seized the pile at the same time, tugging and pulling until it tore in all directions. Sheets of paper flew into the air, like feathers in a breeze, and drifted off around the room, leaving the dazed ofsted exposed, skulking on a pile of maths books. The startled animal curled his lip to show a rack of yellow teeth and shook his long, tangled hair in an attempt to look big and scary. Then he leapt off the desk, shot through a forest of children's legs and fled towards the safety of his cupboard.

Several arms were scrabbling on the floor for their favourite colour of paper, but the movement stopped abruptly on hearing Miss Hazel's voice.

"Children! What is wrong with you this morning? There is plenty of paper for everyone. I am shocked by this horrible behaviour!" The class stared at her in silence, while the offending children slunk back to their seats. In the chaos, no one noticed a small animal, like a tattered, long-nosed and very hairy guinea pig, race away to the cupboard. All he left behind was a mist of fine yellow dust that had been shaken out of his greasy fur.

"I am very disappointed that Year 6 children are not yet able to share with each other," Miss Hazel said simply. The children's hearts sank a little as the twinkle left her eyes and her lips set in a hard line.

"Amy, Emily, please help to clear up this mess," she requested, pointing at the drifts of dusty paper. Bella had already started tidying the paper into piles, while the rest of the class put their heads down and resumed silently cutting, painting and sticking.

Bella stood up with an armful of paper and leant on the desk, feeling rather odd. Glancing around, she noticed Amy and Emily yawning widely, while sluggishly gathering paper on their hands and knees. Very slowly, Amy abandoned the paper she was collecting. With a long sigh, she curled up under a table, placed her thumb in her mouth and sank into a deep sleep. Emily was less fortunate and gently slid forward on her hands until her shoulder caught on a table leg. There she stayed, gently snoring with her cheek pressed to the floor and her bottom in the air, like a terrier with its nose down a rabbit hole. Bella was surprised to find her own mouth stretched in a huge yawn, before sliding gracefully to the floor and landing with an undignified thud.

In small clutches, the children sagged and flopped in their chairs. Some came to rest with their heads on the tables, while others slithered off their chairs into crumpled heaps on the floor. Two girls were surprised when they collapsed across the model of the cliffs of Dover, narrowly avoiding skewering themselves on the ships' masts. Miss Hazel desperately tried to stifle a yawn, looking round in disbelief at her class through what seemed to be a fine yellow haze. She tried to say something sensible, but her thoughts were muffled and disordered. She vaguely wondered how anyone could possibly fall asleep in an art lesson, then sank into a chair near the back of the class. If she could just rest her head on the desk for a moment, she would feel better. Using one arm as a pillow, she drooped forward on to the table to rest her heavy eyes. There she slept, with her wavy hair falling across her shoulder and on down towards the floor.

Silence enveloped Year 6. Break time came and went. The yellow dust settled.

After her fourth cup of coffee, Miss Crimpet felt much better. She began prowling around the school, giving gold stickers to hard-working pupils. She approached Year 6 with a spring in her step but slowed as she became aware of something unusual . . . silence. The corridor would be quiet with Years 4 and 5 not in school, but there was also a Year 6 class on this side of the school. She peered through the glass door into the classroom. Twenty-nine bodies were slumped around the room: twenty-eight children and Miss Hazel. All were fast asleep. There was something strangely malevolent about the scene, as though an evil presence was lurking in the air, waiting to attack anyone foolish enough to try to intervene. Miss Crimpet felt the hairs on her arms prickle as she edged around the door. Amy snored gently near her feet, and Bella was dribbling on to an English book that had fallen to the floor. Miss Crimpet gave Amy a gentle kick and prodded Bella firmly in the ribs, but the class slept on. She stared speechless at the scene.

It felt so wrong to see so many children sleeping, silent, still. The atmosphere felt eerie, dangerous and impossible.

Quietly, she closed the door and snuck away, like a guilty burglar retreating from the scene of a crime. Returning to her office, she closed the door behind her and leant back against it. Her breath came in short, shallow gasps, her hands trembled against the door handle and her mind spun in useless circles. She recognised the signs; the emotion that was coursing through her veins was panic.

Chapter Three

Miss Crimpet stood shaking in her office, with her mind darting off first in one direction and then in another, like a frightened fly trapped in a jar. *What on earth had happened in Miss Hazel's class? How am I going to explain to the parents that the school has put twenty-eight children into a coma? What about the lovely Miss Hazel? She is due to get married in two weeks. Holy Moly! Her fiancé is a massive, muscly Army officer – trained to kill. He might come and snap my legs like a pair of twigs in revenge.* Even in her deranged state, Miss Crimpet had to admit that Miss Hazel's fiancé was a very charming young man, who did not appear to be the type of person to go round snapping legs. However, he was still gigantic and was not going to be keen to marry an unconscious bride.

She reached for a huge bar of chocolate and a small bottle of brandy, which she kept in the bottom drawer of her desk in case of emergencies. She studied the brandy carefully because she did not usually approve of drinking during working hours. However, dealing with twenty-eight unconscious children really was an emergency, so she tipped the contents into her mouth. As the scorching liquid slid down her throat, Miss Crimpet began to consider her options seriously. The pupils did not seem to be unwell, just asleep. It was vital to establish the cause of the problem without creating panic among the other children in the school. She would have to proceed cautiously. *What to*

 DOI: 10.4324/9781003208082-4

do? What to do? She chewed her lip for a while and then grabbed her mobile and dialled Doctor Jeremy Bling.

At 11.23 a.m. a spotless silver car swept into the school car park. Dr Emily Smart checked her watch and noted that, as usual, she was perfectly on time for her 11.30 meeting. Emily Smart was the school psychologist, which meant that it was her job to help solve problems. She had already had a busy morning helping a child who refused to write and one who was too scared to come to school, as well as finding her colleague's earring, which had fallen down the plughole of the office sink. She picked up her bags and glided calmly into Applehurst Primary School, with a magic wand tucked up her sleeve. When she popped her head into Miss Crimpet's office to announce her arrival, she was surprised to find the headteacher shouting at her phone with a large smear of chocolate down one cheek.

"I need you now!" cried the anguished teacher into her mobile, which lay on her desk.

"Well, Bertha, it's very gratifying to know that you find me so hard to resist," replied the phone in a smooth, confident tone. "But I have patients to see this morning. Can't you tame your desires until this evening?" Miss Crimpet flushed purple, briefly catching Emily Smart's eye before the visitor ducked back out of the office and began intently studying the school lunch menu that was pinned to a notice board in the corridor.

"I'm not talking about us," Miss Crimpet hissed at the phone. "This is an exceptional medical emergency. I need your professional opinion, not a smooch behind the bike sheds."

"Ah, I see," said Dr Bling, pausing for a moment, while his professional curiosity overcame his dented ego. "What type of medical emergency?"

"The like of which I've never seen before. Something that needs to be kept quiet to prevent complete panic. You'll have to see it to believe it," came the reply.

"I'll get my things."

"Please! Hurry! I need you!" she urged.

"One hunky hero on his way," purred the phone. Miss Crimpet flinched slightly, frowning at the mobile in distaste, before ending the call.

Dr Smart waited, wide-eyed, in the corridor for a few seconds, trying to comprehend the meaning of the interaction she had overheard. She waited until Miss Crimpet's breathing began to steady and then tapped cautiously on the door and peered at her colleague. Glancing up, Miss Crimpet managed to regain some of her composure.

"Emily. Thank goodness you're here. I need you to see something." She shoved a large chunk of chocolate into her mouth and led the way towards Year 6.

Emily Smart stared at the scene in the classroom, gazing in amazement at the children, many of whom had slid to the floor in piles and were all snoring. Miss Hazel looked as beautiful as ever with her head resting on a table. Two boys were sleeping at the same table, one with his arm submerged in a large bowl of glue.

"You've got to wake them up!" whispered Miss Crimpet.

"Well, what put them to sleep?" murmured Dr Smart, as she peered through the glass in the door.

"How the blazes should I know?" retorted Miss Crimpet. A long pause followed.

"Hmm . . . This is a bit unusual. Surely you need a medical doctor, not a psychologist?" Dr Smart muttered, wishing that the wand up her sleeve was real and not just a toy she had brought to use with the Year 1 class.

"I know, I know. Dr Bling is on his way. Can't you assess them or something? You're supposed to know what to do when odd things happen," begged Miss Crimpet.

"Not when it is this odd, and I do expect children to be conscious when I work with them," replied Dr Smart shortly. "Perhaps it would help if I observed the class?"

They stood together and watched. The class slumbered on.

Chapter Four

Zack Snodgrass let out a heavy, bored sigh. He had regained his breath after having run from the car park. He hated hospital appointments, and here he was again, sitting on the hard chairs in the waiting room, expecting his name to be called. The waiting room – the room where you had to wait while your life ticked past and your friends at school had fun making a model of the Spanish Armada. He kicked his chair leg with the toe of his shoe. His mother sat, still breathing heavily with her handbag clutched in her lap, twisting an exhausted-looking handkerchief between her fingers. He knew that she ought to be at work and that her boss would make her work late to make up the lost time, but here she was at the hospital again with him, loyal and uncomplaining as ever.

This was the fourth time that his hearing had been tested in recent years. There had also been the appointments when his ears had been infected all the time and he had to have an operation to have grommets inserted when he was three. Apparently, they were like tiny pieces of hosepipe inserted into the eardrum, and they helped all the gunge drain out of his inner ear. He knew that the operation had worked because everything had been so loud when he woke up. He could hear the tick of the clock and the rustle of the nurse's uniform. The noise felt sharp, intrusive, unavoidable, whereas before the world had been comfortably muffled and peaceful. So he had screamed

 DOI: 10.4324/9781003208082-5

and that made everything much worse. The sound of his own cries drilled into his head. His mother had been there, clutching his small body to her shoulder, gently rocking his sobs away. She was always there, like a tree that he could cling to whenever he felt that life might blow him away. She was firmly rooted to the ground, dependable and safe. He looked across at her tired face with two neat frown lines etched between her brows. His poor mum; if only he wasn't such a problem, she wouldn't worry so much. He reached across, untangled her hand from the handkerchief and gave it a squeeze. She smiled at him.

"You OK?" she asked.

"I'm OK," he confirmed.

"Good," she said decisively. She squeezed his hand in return and then let it fall. She knew better than to expect him to hold her hand in public for any length of time.

Zack wasn't worried, just bored. He knew that this hearing test would be OK today because he could hear fairly well at the moment. He just couldn't hear well when he got a cold and his ears bunged up.

It wasn't just his ears that caused problems; his eyes had been dodgy, too. It was only when Miss Hazel asked him to describe what writing looked like to him that he realised what he saw was unusually fuzzy. Everyone else had asked him to read the letters, not to describe how they looked, whether they were crisp or blurry, still or moving around. Back in Year 3, Zack often saw two letters on the page, when there was actually only one.

After hearing Zack's description of how the letters looked to him, Miss Hazel had crossed her arms and sat back in her chair.

"I think it is time you saw an optician, young man," she said firmly.

Zack wasn't going to argue with Miss Hazel, even though, at the time, he wasn't sure what an optician was and thought it sounded painful.

The optician had turned out to be a round lady, with large glasses and surprised, fluttery eyes. She did lots of eye tests, many of which involved her bending over and looking closely into his eyes with a bright light. Zack remembered the visit clearly, because twice, when the lady had bent over, she'd let out a little fart, which had made him giggle and made her go pink. She recovered quickly, saying, "I'm so sorry, there seems to be a barking spider in my consulting room today."

"Don't worry, we have plenty of barking spiders at home," Mrs Snodgrass had replied.

"Especially after your onion soup," put in Zack.

"Too much detail, Zachariah," chided his mother, "Now stop giggling, you're making your eyes wobble." But the optician had winked at him, and even Mrs Snodgrass had laughed when it happened again. The optician had given him glasses, which felt odd to begin with, but he had to admit that everything looked much less fuzzy.

Since then, he had to wear reading glasses, and they always fell off when he bent down. His glasses had never quite recovered from the time when Ben had squashed them on to his face while pretending to be an attacking kraken. The glasses did seem to help, but he would have far preferred to have been normal with perfect eyes and ears like most of the children in his class.

Of course, while Zack watched the waiting-room clock endlessly tick the present into the future, he had no idea that the eyes of his classmates were tightly shut as they slumbered the morning away. All except for Ned, who had an unsettling way of sleeping with his eyelids slightly open and his eyes rolled back in his head so that he looked like a demented zombie. Ned would have been delighted with the effect, but unfortunately he was always asleep when it happened and so was unaware of his gruesome habits. He was also unaware, as he lay sleeping on that clement morning, that Ginger Gunge, his most prized slug, had slithered out of his pocket, up his side and was slowly undulating its way across his shoulder.

Chapter Five

Back in school, Miss Crimpet and Dr Smart were still together, intently observing the slumbering Year 6 class. They both jumped when a tall, handsome man flung open the double doors and strode confidently down the corridor. He wore a pink collared shirt that was open at the neck, displaying a tanned chest with a healthy forest of hair. With a black bag in one hand, he ruffled his thick blond hair with the other. Dr Jeremy Bling had arrived.

"Hello, ladies," he announced with a foxy grin. "I see that you are looking as lovely as ever, Bertha." He took Miss Crimpet's hand and slowly kissed the back of it while staring deeply into her eyes. Miss Crimpet giggled and swayed slightly, like a puppet on a string. Dr Smart folded her arms and said nothing, trying to ignore the pungent smell of aftershave that had followed him up the corridor. Dr Bling turned to her and offered a firm, lingering handshake.

"We haven't met, I'm sure I would remember your eyes if we had . . . er . . . Miss . . .?"

"Smart, Dr Smart, Educational Psychologist," Emily shot back, swiftly removing her hand. "And no, we have definitely not met before."

"Ah, I do so like meeting intelligent women," he smirked. Emily secretly hoped that she would never have to meet Dr Bling again. She was glad when he turned his dazzling smile back to Bertha Crimpet, who quickly directed him to look through the glass into the classroom.

 DOI: 10.4324/9781003208082-6

"Great Heavens!" he exclaimed as he took in the scene. "What have you done to them?"

"Nothing," replied Miss Crimpet frostily. "They seem to have done it to themselves."

After the sketchy details of the incident had been discussed, Dr Bling slid on rubber gloves and a face mask, and warily entered the room. He too felt a sense of mystical foreboding about the area, as though he had stumbled on the occupants of an enchanted, sleeping castle. For a moment, he quite fancied playing the role of the gallant prince, particularly as his eyes rested on Miss Hazel, who was sleeping very prettily. If only he could solve the problem by giving her a kiss. Hmm . . . glancing over his shoulder, he saw Miss Crimpet peering through the glass in the door, her lips pursed in anxiety and disapproval. No, he decided, kissing Miss Hazel might cause him to be accused of improper behaviour towards a sleeping patient, rather than making him a hero. Also, although he knew that heroes were required to be brave, he had no intention of doing anything that might put himself in danger. Something had afflicted these children, and he was not going to be infected by it. He had been told that he was not very attractive when he slept. He knew he made odd noises when he breathed out, like the sound of a whale surfacing, and his hair was always stuck to the side of his face in the morning. He ruffled his hair with a gloved hand and determined that he was not going to ruin his image by falling prey to a mysterious sleeping sickness.

He circled the bodies as if he were approaching a den of drowsy tigers. Very cautiously, he listened to Amy's heartbeat, while leaning as far away from her as his stethoscope allowed. He shone a pencil torch into Ned's half-open eyes. Slowly, he ran a finger along one of the desks and inspected the unusual vivid, yellow dust that coated much of the room.

Suddenly, he snapped off the gloves, threw them into the class bin and stepped back into the corridor, shutting the door firmly behind him. He ignored the two waiting women, who looked at him expectantly. Instead, he lounged on a table with his back against the wall and began tapping the keys of his laptop. Time passed.

Zack's bottom had gone numb. He had been sitting on the plastic chair in the waiting room for over an hour, while the nurses regularly emerged, calling patients to join them behind the heavy double doors of the audiology department. There were so many names. After each name there was a scuffling, as the patients scrambled out of their seats, replacing magazines and gathering pushchairs.

"Amy Phelps? . . . Hello, my name is Lucy. Come this way, please."

"Bert Jones? . . . Bert Jones? Ah, Mr Jones, this way, please."

"Toby Hayes? . . . Sorry to keep you waiting. Follow me, please."

"Zachariah Snodgrass?" Zack shot out of his seat, noticing that a teenaged girl had giggled when his name had been called. What had his parents been thinking when they called him Zachariah Snodgrass? It was a silly name for any child, let alone one who could not spell. Zack realised that his parents would not have known that he was unable to spell when he was born, but it was still a silly name. He glared at the girl, who flushed and looked away.

"Zack. My name's Zack," he said hurriedly, following the nurse through the doors.

Mrs Snodgrass glanced again at her watch. She had only had enough change for two hours of parking. They had now been in the hospital for two hours and ten minutes, and she was worried that she would get a parking ticket. The audiologist continued talking about Zack's ears.

"Zack, I'm afraid that your Eustachian tubes are not very well designed, so they don't drain the fluid from your ears as well as normal, which is why you've had so many ear infections and your ears get blocked up so easily."

Mrs Snodgrass tapped her feet. The audiologist was being kind, but they had heard all this before, and everything was taking so long this morning.

"Your hearing is within normal limits today."

"I know," replied Zack ironically, "I can hear you." Mrs Snodgrass gave him a warning look, but the audiologist smiled.

"You've not had an infection for over a year, so I am hopeful that you will grow out of this problem. As the tubes get bigger, they usually drain better." That was good news. Zack let out his breath.

Mrs Snodgrass was poised on the edge of her chair like a coiled spring. Eventually, the audiologist stood and shook her hand. Once in the corridor, Zack's mum began to run.

"Quick, run! We're going to get a parking ticket." Zack bounded down the three flights of stairs, with his mother puffing behind him, clutching her handbag and a wad of leaflets that the audiologist had given them.

They burst out of the main entrance of the hospital. On the far side of the car park, they could see a truck with a small crane. Clamped in the crane was Mrs Snodgrass's car as it swung gently up from the parking space on to the back of the truck.

"Nooooo!" yelled Mrs Snodgrass, lurching across the car park towards her car. "Please put it back! That's my car!" She huffed across the parking lot as fast as she could. Zack hurried after his mother, scooping up leaflets as they fell out of her hand and scattered under parked cars. By the time they arrived, Mrs Snodgrass's car was being strapped on to the truck.

"Please put it back!" called Mrs Snodgrass to the driver, who stared at her blankly.

A great, gangly traffic warden appeared from behind the truck. He was so thin that he looked as if someone had grabbed his head and stretched him like a piece of Blu-tack. He peered at Mrs Snodgrass through little piggy eyes and picked at a large spot on the side of his face.

"I'm sorry, madam," he said, not sounding at all sorry, "but it is too late. Once a car has been lifted, you have to go to the pound to get it back."

"But I'm only a few minutes late, sir," pleaded Mrs Snodgrass.

"Thirty-two minutes late and I'm not called sir, but Traffic Officer Simms," snarled the traffic warden. "And **you** parked in a space reserved for hospital staff."

"No, I didn't," replied Mrs Snodgrass, looking confused. The traffic warden pointed to a small sign with tiny writing saying, *Priority parking for resident registrars. Reservations are to be made through reception*.

"I'm very sorry, Traffic Officer Simms," said Mrs Snodgrass, "But I didn't see the sign. We came back as fast as we could, but the audiologist was running late."

"Not my problem, love," replied the traffic warden unkindly. He thumped on the side of the truck and shouted, "Take it away, Jack," to the driver. He pushed the ticket into Mrs Snodgrass's hands. "You can get it from the car pound on the other side of town. The fee is eighty pounds."

"Eighty pounds!" stammered Mrs Snodgrass. "I don't have eighty pounds." She took the man's arm. "Please, I have to get to work and take my son back to school. Please could you give it back?" A tear ran down her cheek, and her voice trembled as she spoke. "I promise I'll be more careful where I park next time." The truck drove off down the hill.

"You should have looked more carefully **this** time," snapped the traffic warden. Roughly, he shook her off his arm. She stumbled back, tripping on the kerb and landed heavily against a lamp post, bruising her cheek. The traffic warden did not attempt to help her up. Instead, he jabbed his finger at the sign,

"READ . . . THE . . . SIGN!"

Zack ran to help his mother up, wiping her tears on his sleeve. "We can't read the sign," he called after the traffic warden, but he had stalked away. "The words are too long," he mumbled to himself.

Zack's cheeks were burning with shame. It was his fault that they were at the hospital. It was his fault that they had parked in a hurry because he had been slow getting up this morning. Most of all, he should have protected his mother from being pushed over by a spotty giant. Mrs Snodgrass sniffed.

"Thank you, dear. I'm OK. Let's go and find a bus."

Chapter Six

Dr Bling had been draped on the table for over forty minutes, frantically tapping at his laptop. At regular intervals, Miss Crimpet overcame her dread of this situation becoming public and resolved to call the hospital, but each time Dr Bling halted her with sensible comments such as "Not yet" or "Wait another few minutes" or "There's no rush, they're not going anywhere".

He sounded so authoritative that in her panicked state of mind she followed his lead. The truth was that Jeremy Bling had no idea what the problem was, but this was the most interesting medical dilemma he had encountered in his career as a GP. If he solved the mystery, he knew he would appear to be the gallant prince after all. He didn't want a fleet of ambulances from the hospital stealing his thunder and taking charge of his twenty-nine slumbering patients.

Miss Crimpet pulled herself together and stopped any other pupils using the corridor on their way to lunch.

Eventually, after much sighing, Dr Bling gave up on the internet. Delving into the bottom of his bag, he pulled out a tatty old book and began flicking through pages of tiny writing.

Miss Crimpet paced up and down, whispering to herself. Dr Smart called her office to cancel her afternoon appointments.

At last Dr Bling stood up, looking triumphant.

DOI: 10.4324/9781003208082-7

"I've got it! I think I've got it," he finally announced.

"Got what?" muttered Emily Smart irritably. The way his aftershave hung heavily in the air was making her feel queasy.

"It is possibly a Dose of the Yawns, but there's no record of it ever being this nasty before."

"A Dose of the Yawns?" repeated the two women.

"Yes. It is very rare, sometimes found in Eastern Europe. There have been rumours of it occurring in the Carpathian Mountains, where some of the goat herders are unusually sleepy." He slowly read from the ancient medical book: *"A very contagious disease carried via dust mites that live on a few small animals, including shrews, voles and ofsteds. The mites appear to look like bright yellow dust when viewed with the naked eye. Symptoms include repeated yawning and feeling very sleepy. Sometimes people fall asleep and are unable to be woken. There is no known cure, but patients usually make some level of recovery after about six weeks. Those who get better do not remember what happened."*

Miss Crimpet sat on the locker with a thump.

"Six weeks?" she echoed, "That's a catastrophe!"

"How on earth has a Year 6 class caught a disease that is usually found on small mammals in Eastern Europe?" demanded Dr Smart. "It doesn't sound very likely."

Dr Bling gestured to the slumped bodies that littered the classroom. "That doesn't look very likely either, but there they are."

"Oh, great hairy armpits! How will I tell the parents?" Bertha Crimpet exploded. She did not voice her next thought which was *What if I lose my job*? but she suddenly realised just how much she loved Applehurst Primary School and how empty her life would be without it.

"What happens to those who don't recover?" murmured Dr Smart.

"It doesn't say," replied Dr Bling gloomily.

The three professionals stared sadly at the peaceful scene in the classroom, as they realised it was possible that some of the children might never wake again.

Eventually, Dr Smart stated firmly, "It is time we called the hospital and the police."

Miss Crimpet shuddered.

"Yes, we don't have much choice," Dr Bling acknowledged. "But no one should enter the class, or the whole school may become infected. If it is a Nasty Dose of the Yawns, there is no rush to get the children to hospital, because nothing can be done except to make them comfortable until they wake up. However, if the dust spreads, we could have an epidemic on our hands."

Wearily, Miss Crimpet returned to her office and phoned the emergency services. Within an hour the school car park was unusually full. Important-looking men and women in suits scuttled into the school, wondering if Miss Crimpet had gone bonkers. Police, doctors and education officials whispered to each other as they snuck through the school to the meeting room. Although they did not know the details of the disaster, they knew that they must not panic the younger children in the school, who were happily painting, making models and, in the case of one boy, practising his scissor skills by cutting chunks out of the girls' hair.

Dr Bling immediately ordered the police to guard the corridor. He felt terribly important and gave his hair an extra ruffle to impress Miss Crimpet. She was too busy biting her nails to notice. As the suspected disease was so contagious, he insisted that no one was allowed to enter the classroom. He was desperate to collect some dust samples but had to wait for the protective clothing to be dug out of a locked storeroom in the hospital basement. To the embarrassment of the hospital management, the key to the storeroom was missing. It was, in fact, in the pocket of a caretaker called Dave, who was snoozing under a tree while he digested his cheese sandwiches.

Miss Crimpet tried to explain the situation to everyone. The professionals gaped, panicked, planned and re-planned for much of the afternoon. They all dreaded the 3 p.m. deadline when twenty-eight parents would gather outside Year 6, and distress and chaos would be unavoidable. Miss Crimpet let the action plans drift over her as she chewed her way through her final bar of emergency chocolate.

Dr Emily Smart offered several helpful ideas about how best to support the affected families.

Dr Bling waited impatiently for the protective clothing to arrive. He began planning the award-winning research paper that he would write about the incident titled *How the Nastiest Dose of the Yawns ever recorded was conquered*! After that, he began imagining the newspaper articles that would be written about him. *Clever doc rescues school from sleep disease*! and *Dr Bling prevents epidemic*. The articles would be accompanied by his dazzling photo. He thought that his purple shirt would be best for the photo shoot. It would bring out the blue of his eyes. The meeting dragged on. Year 6 slept.

Chapter Seven

Zack waved goodbye to his mother, who watched him head through the school gate before she drove back to work. However, he did not go into the playground but pushed through the hedge and past some trees until he reached a small grassy area, hidden from the school buildings. It had been a rotten morning. He had wasted hours at the hospital waiting to see the audiologist, when it would have been the best day of the school year . . . a whole day of art, which he loved, and no writing, which he hated. The one day when he really wanted to be at school, and he had missed the whole morning.

Flopping down on the grass, Zack stretched out in the sun. It had taken nearly two hours to get the car back. It was lunchtime now, and he felt like eating his lunch alone today. Miss Hazel would not know that he had arrived back in time for lunch. He liked eating with his friends most days, but he did not want to talk about the audiologist or the traffic warden. Miss Hazel said that he had special needs, but he was fed up with being special. Not being able to read and write didn't make him 'special'. It just made people assume he was thick. He hated looking stupid in front of his friends. He hated the way everyone assumed that he would be able to read signs and instructions. Most of all, he hated being told off all the time. He winced at the memory of Miss Crimpet asking him to read out loud in assembly without any warning. He had been so humiliated that he had thrown the

 DOI: 10.4324/9781003208082-8

book at her in front of the whole school. Miss Crimpet had been quite understanding when she realised the problem, but his mother had been furious.

Miss Hazel was different to most of his other teachers. She had a way of making tasks a bit easier for him so that he did not feel overwhelmed. She had suggested that he and his dad read magazines about machines and inventions together. Zack had enjoyed that. He loved learning about how things worked. Miss Hazel suggested he read books electronically. This helped because he could make the writing really large, which made it easier for him to read. She had also shown him how to download audiobooks. They had been amazing. He'd listened to two Harry Potter books already and was about to start the third.

Some of the children still teased him about his writing, but his friend Ben seemed to understand. Miss Hazel allowed them to do paired reading in class so that Ben could help with all the difficult words when they were looking at textbooks. The thought of Ben raised Zack's spirits a bit. Everything seemed easier when you had a really good friend.

He flicked open his lunch box and found a cheese and pickle sandwich, a pear, a banana and a large slab of homemade chocolate cake. He felt sorry for his mum. He knew she would be in trouble at work for being so late. She had carefully looked at all the leaflets that the audiologist had given her, even though Zack knew she couldn't read most of it. That didn't stop her making great cakes, and she always tried to help him. The problem was that, sometimes, he just wanted to be left alone or be the one to **give** help for a change, rather than always being the one needing support. He sank his teeth into the cake and lay in the sun, watching small clouds dance across the sky, not realising that, at that very moment, his friends were in desperate need of his help.

Pear juice dripped down his fingers, so Zack licked them clean and gathered the remains of his lunch into his lunchbox. He had dozed a bit in the sun, and afternoon lessons would have already started. He abandoned his hiding place and pushed through the bushes into the playground. As he was late, he took the shortest route to the classroom through the cloakroom and was surprised to find the door locked. However, the latch on the window in the corner was still broken, and he easily climbed through and headed down the passage to his classroom. Zack did not notice the silence at first, but the sight of a human leg just inside the doorway of the classroom caught his eye. He also became aware of an unpleasant smell, which for some reason reminded him of the health centre next door.

He peered through the door, sidestepping over the leg, and found a jumble of sleeping bodies strewn across the room. Zack quietly closed the door behind him and frowned. What a bizarre sight! No one seemed hurt. He carefully moved further into the room and could see poor Miss Hazel draped across a large table, next to Ben and Ned. Ben had a huge bowl of glue stuck to his elbow. Ned's sweatshirt had several trails of slime leading up his torso and on to the table.

It was then that Zack spotted the large ginger slug, quite well camouflaged on the wood-effect table-top, making steady progress towards Miss Hazel's face. Zack did not usually freak out about bugs, but he had an extreme dislike of slugs ever since Ned had hidden one in his ham sandwich. He cringed at the memory of finding his sandwich chewier than expected and the horrible feeling as the slug had slid down his throat whole before he even knew what it was. Ned had been furious and told everyone that Zack had deliberately eaten his best friend. Only Ned could be best friends with a slug, thought Zack moodily.

Enraged by the thought of the ill-mannered slug oozing its way up Miss Hazel's face, Zack tried to summon the courage to pick the slug up in his fingers. Then he had an excellent idea. He made for the cleaning cupboard. It was clear that something weirdly serious had happened to the rest of the class, and so Zack decided to take precautions. He did not like the look of the bright yellow dust, which almost seemed to glow on every surface. He pulled on a pair of pink rubber gloves and tied a clean duster over his nose and mouth. At least that helped keep out the horrid smell, which he was still struggling to identify. He returned to the class pushing a vacuum cleaner. The machine buzzed energetically and by carefully aiming the nozzle, Zack dragged the slug from the table with a small satisfying splat. In an effort to reduce the slime trail, he kept the nozzle trained on the ooze just below Miss Hazel's nose and was surprised to see a small yellow cloud of dust emerge from her nostrils and follow the unhappy slug into the vacuum cleaner. Two more slugs were heading towards Ben, and Zack enjoyed the "splat, splat" as they shot up the tube and began spinning around inside the cylinder.

Once again, as the nozzle came near Ben's face, a small yellow cloud slid out of his nose and down the nozzle. *Hmm . . . Interesting,* thought Zack, who soon sucked a yellow cloud from Ned's nose as well.

He turned off the vacuum cleaner and prepared to go and find some help when Miss Hazel stretched and peered at him with bleary eyes. Zack was suddenly embarrassed by the fact he was wearing pink rubber gloves and a yellow facemask, but he tried to act as normally as possible.

"Are you all right, Miss Hazel?" he asked, "I think you've had a bit of a snooze."

"I'm fine," replied the befuddled teacher, wondering about the awful smell that was dominating her classroom. "Have I really been asleep?"

"It is a very warm day. I think everyone drifted off for a bit. You just sit there and come to, while I help tidy up," replied Zack, looking at the mess of dust, torn tissue paper and sleeping bodies. Ned and Ben began to stir. Ned instinctively felt in his pocket and soon realised something was missing, but for the moment he could not remember what.

Zack was quick to see the importance of the yellow clouds of dust. He whipped around hoovering up small yellow clouds from each nose in the room and then sucked up all the dust from the furniture and floor for good measure. Vacuuming proved to be good fun, so he did a really thorough job. *Perhaps I ought to help Mum with the housework more often*, he mused. The tissue paper on the floor was covered in dust and badly torn, so he bundled it up and shoved it in the big bins outside the cloakroom. He found a large bottle of juice and a packet of biscuits left over from a Christmas party, and dished out a drink and a biscuit to his confused classmates. He peeled most of the glue off Ben's elbow. Last of all, he un-squashed the white cliffs of Dover, washed the rubber gloves and returned them to the cleaning cupboard.

By this time, it was 2.50 p.m. and many parents were already chatting outside the classroom door.

"Everyone seems very tired, Miss Hazel. Why don't you let us go a bit early today?" suggested Zack.

Still rather bemused, Miss Hazell agreed to the suggestion. Year 6 gathered their coats and bags and gradually filtered away home, mumbling that school had been 'Fine' as always and not really able to explain why their packed lunches were untouched. Zack was just leaving the classroom when a sudden thought sent him hurrying back to the cleaning cupboard. Here, he carefully emptied the contents of the vacuum cleaner into the sealable plastic bag that had originally contained his sandwiches. He hid this in his rucksack.

"Goodbye, Miss Hazel. Have a good evening," he called over his shoulder. He crossed the playground with a spring in his step and caught the hand of his little sister, who flew towards him from the Year 2 classroom. His mother stood sagging at the edge of the playground, with a livid bruise darkening one cheek.

"Hello, lovelies, you're looking spritely," she said with a weak, sad smile. "I just came to drop you home and then I need to go back to work. My boss has said I have got to make up the time I spent at the car pound today."

"I'm sorry, Mum. I'll cook supper, so it's ready when you get home."

"Bless you, Zack. That would be great. Although, I think it will just be beans on toast tonight. After the cost of getting the car back, I'm afraid there's no money to go to the shops." Zack took his mother's hand and gave it a squeeze.

"Don't worry, Mum. I have a feeling that things might be about to look up." Mrs Snodgrass raised an eyebrow at her son and could not help smiling when she saw the sparkle in his eyes.

Chapter Eight

Dave, the hospital caretaker, had finished digesting his lunch and was surprised to find the head of the hospital administration threatening to break down the door to his storeroom. She grabbed the key, muttering about a biological emergency. By 2.30 p.m. a team of paramedics from the hospital had arrived at the school and were squeezed into Miss Crimpet's office, while they made final adjustments to their protective clothing. At 2.55 p.m. the Head of Children's Services reluctantly emerged from the committee room with a plan in hand. He was flanked by Miss Crimpet and the Chief Constable.

Dr Smart and a handpicked selection of police officers were waiting, ready to support distraught parents. At the same time, three paramedics cautiously advanced up the corridor, their rubber boots squeaking on the tiled floor. Their breathing was heavy and menacing through their masks, and their protective suits rustled with every move. Their hearts were beating fast, as they dreaded witnessing the catastrophe that was about to unfold. Very carefully, they turned the door handle and the door swung inwards.

DOI: 10.4324/9781003208082-9

Before them lay the most extraordinarily normal scene. It was a typical primary school classroom, with sunny display boards and a large round clock in the centre of the far wall. The tables were in neat clusters with chairs tucked beneath them. At the front of the class, a graceful, slender woman sat behind the teacher's desk, with a mug clasped in her hands. She was looking out of the window and frowning at the police cars and ambulances that were discreetly parked in the staff car park.

She turned, hearing the door squeak on its hinges and gave a small yelp, dropping her mug as her arms shot up into the air in surprise. The open doorway was blocked by three alien creatures, peering at her through steamy visors. They breathed with rushing mechanical whooshes, breaking the silence. The three paramedics and the teacher stared at each other in total confusion.

Eventually, a disembodied voice came from the alien on the left.

"Are you all right, miss?"

"I'm fine," replied Miss Hazel crossly, mopping at a pile of exercise books on her desk. "Well, I was fine until you frightened the bejeezus out of me and made me spill my drink."

"We thought you had a Nasty Dose of the Yawns," said the alien on the right.

"A nasty dose of the what?" asked Miss Hazel.

"Yawns," replied the middle alien, removing her face mask and so transforming herself into a perfectly normal paramedic in a protective suit.

"Well, I had a snooze, but I think to send three paramedics in hazmat suits is a bit of an overreaction, don't you?" replied Miss Hazel.

"Not to mention two dozen police officers, the Head of Children's Services and eleven ambulances," said the paramedic on the left, also removing his visor.

"Good Lord!" cried Miss Hazel, "What on earth has been going on?"

"That is exactly what I would like to know!" thundered Miss Crimpet entering the classroom by the playground door, with Dr Bling and the Chief Constable following behind.

"Have you and your pupils been playing some kind of dreadful joke on me all day, pretending to be asleep?"

"No, of course not. We were making a model of the Spanish Armada and . . . " Miss Hazel trailed off, unable to explain what had actually happened for the rest of the day.

Her mind was completely fuzzy. She vaguely remembered Zack tidying up a mess, but nothing was clear enough to make sense. All she knew was that she was tired and keen to go home.

The three paramedics shrugged and rustled off down the corridor to remove their suits. The Chief Constable marched out to stand down all his police officers.

Miss Hazel had been looking forward to an early night and was not pleased when Dr Bling insisted on an in-depth medical examination. As he leant uncomfortably close to examine her eyes, she finally realised that the unpleasant smell dominating her classroom was his sickening aftershave. He then spent a long time scrabbling about on the floor, muttering about yellow dust, but not a speck was to be found. Miss Hazel's temper began to unravel when she was interrogated by the Chief Constable. He asked question after question and became increasingly rude.

"So, Miss Hazel, are you expecting me to believe that your whole class fell asleep mid-morning and woke up at the end of the school day?"

"Yes, that seems to be the case. I am afraid I do not remember anything else."

"Do you usually allow your pupils to sleep for four hours a day?"

"Of course not. Don't be absurd."

"Is your teaching so terrible that they just can't stay awake?" Miss Hazel stared silently back at him, a look of total misery on her face. Dr Bling was still on his hands and knees, searching for dust under the cupboards. Miss Crimpet came to her rescue.

"How dare you insult the quality of Miss Hazel's teaching. She is an excellent and dedicated professional. Whatever happened here today was not her fault."

The Chief Constable fixed Miss Crimpet and Dr Bling's bottom with a steely glare.

"Well, it was *someone's* fault! I am beginning to think that this afternoon has been some kind of sick joke. *A Nasty Dose of the Yawns* indeed! What a ridiculous diagnosis! We will be the laughingstock of the county when this gets out." He snorted in disgust and stomped off towards his car.

Jeremy Bling slowly stood up with a sigh and peeled off his latex gloves. His visions of being a handsome hero had burst like a balloon. He was left with the hideous reality that he had made a complete fool of himself. The headteacher and doctor stood in silence for a moment, while they both wondered how a perfectly normal day had changed into a humiliating mystery. If only they could awake from this bad dream to find that all was well.

"Well . . . umm . . . best be off," muttered Dr Bling sheepishly. "Goodbye, Bertha, Miss Hazel." He slowly backed away towards the door, as if Miss Crimpet might be tempted to pounce on him once he turned his back.

"After what has happened today, I think it's best if we don't go out for dinner tomorrow night, Jeremy," Miss Crimpet said primly. Miss Hazel slid over to the sink in the corner and busied herself washing mugs, suddenly realising that Miss Crimpet's relationship with Jeremy Bling was more intimate than she had assumed.

Dr Bling looked baffled. He had always supposed that women found him irresistible, and yet he had a nasty feeling that he was about to be dumped.

"If you really think that would be best?" He raised his voice at the end of the sentence to make it sound like a question.

"I do think it's best. We are obviously not as well suited as I thought."

"I see," he said slowly. He lingered in the doorway for a few seconds, absorbing the information. Then, feeling that there was nothing left to say, he turned and began walking slowly away. But Betha Crimpet had not quite finished with him.

"One last thing, Jeremy," she commanded in her most headmistressy tone of voice.

"Yes?" he replied hopefully.

"You need to seriously rethink your use of aftershave."

Dr Bling seemed unable to comprehend the meaning of this comment. He had used large quantities of *Mixed Spice,* his favourite brand for years, and had always assumed that it made him extra alluring.

"What's wrong with it?" he asked.

Miss Crimpet appeared reluctant to answer his question. He looked so crestfallen that she didn't have the heart to end the relationship with a direct insult. Instead, she responded with silence, her lips drawn into a thin line.

"What's the matter with it?" he asked again, not taking the hint. Miss Hazel looked up from washing the mugs, quickly glancing at the headteacher and then looking towards the doctor. She decided that for the sake of his patients' sense of smell, it was her duty to intervene.

"It absolutely stinks," she replied.

Chapter Nine

When Zack arrived home, he waved his mother goodbye, checked that his sister was playing happily in the garden and then swiftly set to work. He was fairly sure that he had made a medical discovery that afternoon. He had found a cure for a strange sleeping illness, caused by yellow dust, and he had evidence that this disease did not affect slugs.

"It's time to do an experiment," he mused, rubbing Pebble's ears. The dog blinked lovingly at him. "I'm sorry, Pebble, but I need you to try something. It is all in aid of medical science." Pebble wagged her tail and looked delighted.

He found a pair of his mother's washing-up gloves, an old respirator that his dad used to wear in the Army and a large box of chocolates that Aunt Joan had given him a couple of days ago. He also found a syringe with a sharp needle that his father had used to inject Pebble when she had injured her leg. He knew that his parents would not approve of him playing with medical needles, but this was work and not play, and he would be very careful. He put on the respirator and gently emptied the dirt from the vacuum cleaner on to a tray.

The slugs swayed about drunkenly, and he used the gloves to rinse them off and dump them in a box with some leaves. Then he separated out as much dirt as possible by using a sieve from the

DOI: 10.4324/9781003208082-10

kitchen until he was left with a slightly murky mound of yellow dust. He put most of this into a small freezer bag and sealed it. He mixed the remaining dust with a few drops of water to make a thick paste. Very carefully he put a tiny spot of paste on to a dog biscuit and handed it to Pebble. She helpfully gobbled it down and watched eagerly, hoping for more.

Spooning the paste into the syringe was fiddly because the rubber gloves were too big. *Hmm*, he pondered, *I must get out of the habit of rubber gloves. Twice in one day is weird.* At least these were not pink.

He had been concentrating so hard that he had not noticed that his right foot was unusually warm. Looking down, he saw Pebble slumped across his feet, like a melted ice cream, her cheeks vibrating on each out-breath. He waved a biscuit under her nose and called her name, but she remained a contented, slumbering blanket beneath the table. *Excellent*, he thought. *It works when eaten, as well as when inhaled.*

The only problem was he did not know how to stop it working. He could not suck it out of her tummy with a vacuum cleaner. He would just have to monitor her. If the worst came to the worst, he would find a way to make her sick.

At last, the syringe was full of the hideous yellow paste, and it was time to unwrap the chocolates. He did this with care and slowly lifted out each chocolate. He injected a small amount of yellow paste into the middle of each one. Then he replaced the lid and tied it shut with a large gold ribbon.

Now for the note. This was more difficult because he hated writing, but the box had to have a grown-up-looking note for his plan to work. Zack wasted several pieces of paper with false starts. He managed to get most of the words down, but some of them looked wrong and he wasn't sure how they should be spelt.

Come on, come on, he said to himself. *I can do this. I'm smart; I can conquer The Kraken!* He thought for a while longer. If only he could make it look less childish. Of course, he could use his dad's computer!

Zack was woken the next day by a warm tongue licking his nose. He smiled as he found himself eyeball to eyeball with Pebble. The dog's eyes appeared to be looking in slightly different directions, but her tail was wagging, and she did not seem to have been distressed by her sleepy night. She turned and stumbled into the doorframe. On her second attempt, she made it through the doorway and wobbled away down the corridor. *Poor Pebble,* thought

Zack. *No more rubber gloves and no more experimenting on pets*, he vowed. But he couldn't help grinning as he bounded out of bed.

At breakfast, he asked his mother if he could take the bus into town after school because he needed to go to the library with Ben. Mrs Snodgrass looked at her son indulgently. He had a spring in his step this morning and seemed excited about seeing Ben, but she suspected that a mischievous plan was whizzing around his brain as well.

She thought back to the thunderous ball of anger he had been when he was younger, and the battles she had fought to encourage him to complete his homework. So now to hear that he was voluntarily going to the library made her feel calm and fuzzy, like breathing the scent of freshly mown hay. She sympathised with his frustrations because she had suffered in the same way. She understood only too well the burning humiliation of struggling to read and write in a society that assumes all adults are literate. Each day presented different challenges for her – reading instructions on a packet of medicine, completing forms sent home from school, hiding her failures, tolerating people's ridicule and maintaining her self-respect. She desperately wanted to protect her son from the misery that she had experienced but didn't have the skills to support him.

Thank goodness for Miss Hazel. She had given Zack the determination to succeed. Now, instead of having a battle over homework, mother and son were learning together. They sat at the kitchen table practising the spelling patterns that Miss Hazel had sent home and struggling through his reading books, taking turns to read each paragraph.

Nowadays, it was hard to know if the mother was helping the son or vice versa. One thing was for sure; Zack's dad helped them both with a patience that was surprising, given his zest for life. It was just a shame that he was so often away from home due to his work. She realised that increasingly she relied on Zack during her husband's absences. Just in the last week he had mended a leaky tap, pumped up the car tyres and removed a splinter from Pebble's paw. It was a shame Zack had not been tall enough to tackle that awful traffic warden. Eugh! He had been so rude that it made her want to punch him on the nose.

Zack was busy spooning cereal into his mouth, but he was watching her, clearly expecting a reply about his request to go to the library.

"That's fine, lovie. Why do you need to go to the library?" she asked, slightly suspicious that it sounded too good to be true.

"We have to find out about renewable fuels. Ben and I are trying to design a car that won't pollute the world. We can work on the library computers together after school."

"That's a good idea. Of course, you can go. Try to be back by six, because Dad is coming home tonight."

"No worries, Mum. I'll be back," replied Zack.

What Zack had told his mother was actually true. He did need to go to the library with Ben. However, there was something he had not mentioned. He was pretty sure that the library was next to the Traffic Officers' Headquarters. He planned to pay Traffic Officer Simms a visit on the way.

It was an odd day at school. Miss Crimpet lurked anxiously in the corridor outside Year 6. Zack kept seeing her peeping into the classroom as if she expected something extraordinary to be happening. The children all seemed tired, and Miss Hazel lacked her usual energy. However, they enjoyed completing the model of the Spanish Armada and had the 'funeral' for the class hamster that had been planned for the day before. Ned spent much of the morning moaning about three of his favourite slugs escaping but miraculously found them in his bag at lunchtime, tucked up in a box full of leaves. Towards the end of the day, Miss Hazel called the class together and talked through their ideas for machines that ran off renewable energy.

"In your pairs, have a good think about how your machine will work. We will start drawing plans for them in the morning. Right, everyone, time to pack up. Zack, please may I have a word before you go?"

Zack shuffled reluctantly towards Miss Hazel. He was itching to leave school and did not want to answer any awkward questions about yellow dust, vacuum cleaners or slugs.

"Zack, I just wanted to thank you for helping to clear up yesterday afternoon."

"That's OK," he mumbled.

"This might sound odd, but did you notice anything unusual when you got back yesterday?"

"No," he replied, not quite able to meet her eye. "The room was a mess, and everyone seemed a bit sleepy, but it was a very warm afternoon."

"Indeed, it was . . . very warm," she murmured, frowning to herself. Then she took a deep breath. "Have a good evening, Zack. I'm looking forward to seeing the car that you and Ben are designing tomorrow."

"Goodbye, Miss Hazel. See you tomorrow," replied Zack as he dashed for the cloakroom before she could ask any more questions. Ben was waiting for him.

"Come on, let's go," said Zack. "I'm on a mission!"

"What kind of a mission?" asked Ben.

"You'll see," smiled Zack.

Chapter Ten

They hopped off the bus in the middle of town and headed towards the library. However, Zack stopped outside a grey concrete building with a large sign above its revolving door.

"Traffic Officers' Headquarters," Ben read, "What are we doing here?"

"I'll tell you in a minute," Zack replied mysteriously. He pushed his way around the revolving door and approached the reception desk.

"How can I help you?" asked the middle-aged woman behind the desk, without looking up from the magazine she was reading. Her nametag read *Miss Dint*. She did not sound as though she wanted to help with anything, and

 DOI: 10.4324/9781003208082-11

Zack noticed that her mouth turned down at the corners, which made her look like a disgruntled fish.

"I would like to leave something for Traffic Officer Simms," said Zack bravely.

"Leave it on the side over there," ordered the woman, still not looking up. Zack did as he was told and quickly left the building. After all, it was probably best if no one looked at him too closely.

"Why on earth are you giving presents to traffic wardens?" asked Ben.

"Anyone as rude as Traffic Officer Simms deserves a little surprise," replied Zack. "I just hope it works. I'll tell you all about it at the library."

Traffic Officer Simms was having a very good day. He had issued a record number of tickets and managed to get six cars taken to the car pound. The pregnant woman with the two toddlers had made a bit of a fuss when her car was towed away, but it wasn't his fault that she had parked with the back of her car outside the parking space. *She probably needs some exercise, so a walk across town to the car pound won't do her any harm,* he thought to himself.

"There's a parcel for you, Bernard," Miss Dint grunted, as he sidled into the Traffic Officers' Headquarters. Traffic Officer Simms narrowed his piggy eyes and stared at the box. It looked like a box of fancy chocolates, tied with a large gold ribbon. Gingerly, he lifted out the typed note, which was tucked under the ribbon. It read:

Dear Traffic Officer Sims,

Please except these chocolates as a thank you for all your hard work. I hope you enjoy them.

With best wishes,
A happy member of the community.

Bernard Simms's face broke into an unpleasant grin, which showed a row of pointy, stained teeth. *This really is the best day ever,* he thought. He liked chocolates, even if the sender had missed out an "m" in his name and could not spell 'accept'. *Honestly, what numpty would write 'except' when it should be 'accept'?* He pulled off the lid and swiftly stuck a square piece of chocolate fudge into his mouth. *Mmm, delicious.* He chewed it down and grabbed a round one as he pushed through the door to the traffic wardens' common room. To his dismay, he realised that every traffic warden in Greenford was already there, waiting for their weekly meeting.

"All right, Bernard. What you got there?" asked a cheery, round woman called Daisy. She was very large, with a kind, pleasant face and twinkly eyes. She gazed at the chocolates in the open box, and then exclaimed loudly so that everyone could hear, "Aww, Bernard, you shouldn't have! How kind of you to bring chocolates for us all. That will perk us all up after a long day."

Bernard Simms had not planned on sharing his prize with anyone, let alone the whole department. But he could see eighteen pairs of eyes looking longingly at the box in anticipation.

Bother, blast and codswallop, he thought. With a repellent leer, he passed the box to Daisy, quickly taking a third chocolate on the way. He watched in despair as the box was handed round the room and everyone took one, acknowledging him with smiles and thanks. When the box returned, there were only five chocolates left. Bernard shuffled over to a chair in the corner and guzzled down the remaining chocolates as fast as he could before anyone could ask for more.

"Right, listen in everyone," ordered the head traffic warden. "We are here today to discuss the traffic controls for the funfair tomorrow night. This is intended to be an amusing evening, but I will not have the streets brought to a standstill by families parking all over my yellow lines."

"Hear, hear," and "Quite right," came the murmured agreements from around the room.

"You must all be here from 6 p.m.," continued the head warden, "and . . ."

Bernard Simms did not hear what was said next. He started feeling very strange, as if his body was going to sleep from the inside out. His tummy went numb, so he reached down and prodded his scrawny belly to check it was still there. His arms and legs felt heavy and floppy. The room appeared to be surging from side to side. He tried to stand up, lurched off his chair and stood swaying in the middle of the room. The crash stopped the head warden's drone about parking tickets. Traffic Officer Simms had sprawled on to the coffee table, sending a shower of cold coffee and cardboard cups across the room. His colleagues were stunned and stared at the sleeping form in silence, ignoring the coffee that dripped down their uniforms. Bernard Simms let out a huge shuddering snore from the plate of stale egg sandwiches in which his face was resting.

Eventually, Daisy cried out, "Cor blimey, sir! Do you think he's all right?" But her question went unanswered. The head traffic warden was slumped in his seat and the rest of her colleagues were sliding to the floor, forming a slumbering heap on the sticky grey carpet tiles.

"What on earth . . .?" questioned Daisy. She was the only person left standing. Being rather larger than her fellow traffic wardens, the yellow powder took slightly longer to have an effect. But she did not remain upright for long. Soon her legs began to wobble, and she tottered over with a soft splat and rolled on to several unfortunate colleagues.

Chapter Eleven

About an hour later, Miss Dint looked at her watch. It was 5 p.m. exactly and so she snapped shut her magazine. Her contract stated that she worked 9 a.m. to 5 p.m., so she did not plan to stay a minute longer at the reception desk, even if the traffic wardens' meeting had not finished. She put her magazine into her bag and stomped into the common room.

"I'm off. You can lock up yourselves," she barked before stomping out again. It was only when she was halfway across the lobby that her mind took in what she had seen. Cautiously, she returned to the common room and pushed open the door. Before her lay a heap of bodies, some curled up, others with arms and legs thrown wide. Some were looking uncomfortably squashed under Daisy, who lay at the top of the pile like a contented jellyfish. Her head was thrown back and a line of dribble oozed from the corner of her mouth.

"Grrr, why does this sort of thing always happen when it's time for me to go home?" grumbled Miss Dint, as though she often found all her co-workers in a coma. She plodded back to the reception desk and thumped 999 into the phone.

"I need ambulances for nineteen bodies at the Traffic Officers' Headquarters, and tell them not to park on the double yellow lines," she growled into the phone. "Well, how on earth should I know what's wrong with them? I'm just the receptionist. It's not my job to diagnose medical

DOI: 10.4324/9781003208082-12

complaints." There was a pause while a perplexed emergency worker tried to obtain some more details from the unhelpful Miss Dint. "I can't put them on the phone. They're all unconscious . . . Yes, nineteen of them," she stated firmly before hanging up. She did not really like any of the traffic wardens and felt that it was not her job to see if they were all right. None of them looked ill, she reasoned, just asleep. She settled back behind her desk, reopened the magazine and waited for the tell-tale sirens that would announce the arrival of the emergency services.

Zack and Ben had had an excellent hour or so in the library, and the design of their car was well underway. Zack had explained the scene at the hospital with the traffic warden pushing his mum into a lamp post, the yellow powder, the slugs and the hoover. He chose not to mention the pink rubber gloves.

Ben loved the idea of injecting the yellow paste into the chocolates. "What dose do you need for it to work?" he asked.

"Well, I don't know exactly," said Zack, suddenly feeling a bit worried. "A tiny spot knocked Pebble out for a whole night. So I suppose one chocolate might knock him out for a few days. Anyway, whatever happens, this is our secret forever, remember."

"Forever," replied Ben.

On the way home, the boys were chatting happily on the bus when it suddenly swerved off the road and waited, engine throbbing on the pavement. An ambulance came screaming the other way, followed by another and another. Sirens blared from across the town, all heading towards the centre.

"Ooops," Zack giggled. "I think it might have worked!" But suddenly he became serious. "Hang on, why would they need more than one ambulance?"

"Perhaps he shared the chocolates?" suggested Ben. Zack looked horrified.

"Blimey! I didn't think of that. I didn't mean for anyone else to be affected. I just thought he'd have one chocolate and go to sleep."

"Maybe we'd better listen to the local news tonight and find out what's going on," said Ben.

"Yeah. Good idea. This experiment might have got a bit out of hand." Zack was now seriously worried.

"Well, whatever happens, remember, it is our secret forever," Ben reminded him.

"Yes, forever," agreed Zack.

Chapter Twelve

"Good morning. It's seven o'clock on Friday the 9th of May. The headlines this morning. All members of Greenford's Traffic Enforcement Department are being treated in hospital, after being found comatose in the Traffic Officers' Headquarters last night. The condition of the nineteen traffic wardens has baffled doctors, who say that they appear to be suffering from a serious sleeping sickness that has left them unconscious. However, no cause for their symptoms has been found. Concerns have been raised that their condition may be contagious, particularly after a local GP claimed that they were experiencing 'a Nasty Dose of the Yawns'. Dr Jeremy Bling, of the Applehurst Surgery, stated that 'The Yawns' is a rare affliction, sometimes found in the Carpathian Mountains. He claims that it is caused by small mites that look like vibrant yellow dust. Dr Bling also claims that there was a similar incident at Applehurst Primary School, the children of one class were allegedly rendered unconscious for most of the school day on Wednesday of this week. However, Miss Crimpet, Applehurst's Headteacher has not confirmed Dr Bling's allegations and no sign of the 'yellow dust' has been found either at the school or at the Traffic Officers' Headquarters. However, a parent at the school has reported that there were several police cars and an ambulance in the school's staff car park on Wednesday afternoon. Miss Crimpet has declined to comment.

 DOI: 10.4324/9781003208082-13

"Dennis Winterborne, Greenford's Chief Constable, has suggested that Dr Bling may be the leader of an elaborate hoax. A hospital spokesman confirmed that all the traffic wardens are in a stable condition. It is hoped that they will be able to shed light on the cause of their illness when they awake in due course. In the meantime, council officials are calling for the public to park sensibly, while alternative arrangements can be made for traffic enforcement.

"In other news . . ."

Zack turned off the radio and put his head in his hands. What had he done? Nineteen people were in hospital, because he had had an impulse to take revenge on Traffic Officer Simms, who had only been doing his job – although he had certainly been doing his job in a very unpleasant manner.

"Glory be! Zack! Zack!" called Mrs Snodgrass from downstairs. "Zack! Have you heard the news? All the traffic wardens have been taken ill! That must include that awful oaf we encountered at the hospital."

"Traffic Officer Simms," confirmed Zack dolefully, entering the kitchen.

"Yes. Him. Oh, Zack!" she cried, dancing around the kitchen table. "It seems like divine retribution. He was so horrid. He made me feel stupid and he bruised my face. I know I shouldn't wish others ill, but I'm so delighted." She emphasised her point by waving her wooden spoon at him. "I hope he sleeps for a week!"

Zack couldn't help laughing as his mother skipped around like a little girl, although he was still feeling a bit shaken by the news. *I just hope that he **only** sleeps for a week,* he thought guiltily.

Mrs Snodgrass suddenly stopped skipping and placed her hands on her hips.

"The news said there was also an incident at the school on Wednesday. You didn't see anything odd?" Zack quickly leant into the cereal cupboard, pretending to ponder which type of cereal to have to breakfast. He knew he was blushing, and he did not want to be interrogated by his mother. She might make him go to the police if she knew the awful thing he had done.

"No. Nothing odd," he replied from the cupboard. Mrs Snodgrass took note of the way that his ears were glowing like beacons on the side of his head. No one would ever need to give her son a lie detector test, she thought. His burning ears always showed when he was being deceitful. He emerged from the cupboard, swiftly reaching for a bowl, followed by the milk.

"Zachariah Snodgrass," she said suspiciously, wagging her wooden spoon in his direction, "did you make any children ill on Wednesday?"

"No! Of course not," he replied truthfully. "Anyway, how could I have done? I was with you all morning."

"Well . . . If someone has taken Traffic Officer Simms off the streets for a bit, I'm delighted," she said, smiling broadly. "It has stopped me wishing that I'd punched him on the nose." Zack resumed breathing, grateful that the questioning had stopped there. He was therefore not prepared for his mother's next question.

"Isn't the Traffic Officers' Headquarters next to the library?" she asked innocently. Zack began spluttering into his cereal, aware that his ears were now pulsing red like massive warning lights on a distressed spacecraft. Mrs Snodgrass observed her son's discomfort, slowly laying down her wooden spoon. "At least Pebble has recovered from her very sleepy night."

Zack gasped and inhaled a Shreddie. How did his mother always seem to know his crimes? He had been so careful to put everything away before she returned from work, although he had to admit that the way Pebble had slept through the evening, spread across the floor like a hearth rug, had been suspicious. He reckoned that they must issue mothers with superpowers shortly after the birth of their children, which allowed them always to keep one step ahead of their troublesome offspring.

"Luckily for you," Mrs Snodgrass said to her son, "I think it is better if there are some things in life that I don't know about. I suspect that the cause of the sleeping traffic wardens is one of them."

After it was announced that all Greenford's traffic wardens were receiving emergency treatment at the hospital, the local people went to town. They parked on pavements and double yellow lines. A heavily pregnant woman with two toddlers even left her car half up the steps of the Traffic Officers' Headquarters. No one paid and displayed in the car parks, and a pair of farmers left their tractors in the middle of the High Street, while they enjoyed a pint of fine ale at the pub. Everyone who was caught up in the resulting traffic jam hooted and tooted in protest, and then abandoned their cars and joined the farmers in the pub. Mrs Snodgrass joined the jovial throng on the High Street during her lunch hour. She sat in the sun with a glass of sherry in one hand and a succulent bacon butty in the other.

"I've not had this much fun in years!" she chuckled to a friend, through a mouthful of butty.

After a morning of happy chaos, the Army was called in to restore order and to manage the parking at the funfair that evening. The soldiers mingled with the crowd during the funfair, directing traffic with a cheerfulness that had not been seen in Greenford for many years.

Dr Bling was kept busy up at the hospital experimenting on the traffic wardens. He had appointed himself as an expert on Doses of the Yawns and therefore insisted on taking charge of the sleeping patients. He became so self-important that the hospital staff stopped taking him seriously and began to laugh openly at his ridiculous claims about a Nasty Dose of the Yawns. He spent hours searching the unconscious patients for yellow dust, but none was found. For several weeks he observed, examined, tested, prodded and scrutinised the comatose patients, convinced that he would find a cure for this second attack, but they provided him with no evidence or explanations, preferring to sleep in dreamy peace.

The first to recover was Daisy, after three weeks of contented slumber. One by one, the other wardens woke up, feeling confused but refreshed. To Dr Bling's annoyance, none of them was able to give any helpful information about what had caused the incident. Their relieved families reported that they had returned home in a positive mood and resumed their old lives with more cheerfulness than had previously been the case. Gradually, Jeremy Bling's tan faded under the hospital lights and his hair grew thinner due to his habit of ruffling it whenever a pretty nurse passed his way. As the eighteenth traffic warden left the hospital, he had to admit that he had no idea what had caused or cured the outbreak. He slunk back to his usual role at the health centre, unable to take credit for what had been a brilliant and accurate diagnosis.

It was six months before Traffic Officer Simms awoke. He had a lot of time to reflect as he regained his strength. He soon realised that something about the chocolates had sent him to sleep. However, he did not want to admit that he had been so disliked that someone had tried to poison him. Nor did he want to admit that he was so greedy that he had eaten eight chocolates when everyone else had only had one. So, he did not share his suspicions with the hospital staff. He eventually returned to work in a slightly more relaxed and generous frame of mind.

The mystery of the sleeping traffic wardens remained unsolved.

Life at Applehurst Primary School continued unin-terrupted. No one spoke of the unusual Wednesday when something odd might have happened. As no one was quite sure what it was, and as Miss Crimpet deftly avoided any questions relating to sleeping at school, there was nothing to discuss. Now that she was not distracted by the attentions of Dr Bling, Miss Crimpet returned to being an efficient and dedicated headteacher. She took up running with a local club in the evenings and enjoyed exploring new routes around the nearby countryside. She became particularly friendly with a flower farmer, who rescued her when she sprained her ankle in his tulip field.

Since that day Miss Crimpet's office overflowed with flowers. A school vegetable garden was created and riotous flowerbeds appeared around the school grounds. Miss Crimpet glowed.

Miss Hazel married her enormous, muscled fiancé. She continued teaching after a brief but adventurous honeymoon in the Scottish Highlands over half-term. On returning to school, she felt that she could no longer ignore the unpleasant smell that lurked in the back of her art cupboard.

One Friday afternoon, when all the children had gone home, she gathered a large bin and a range of cleaning materials and set to work. She spotted the old hamster cage lying open in a corner and was overcome with guilt that she had not replaced the class hamster as she had intended. She was surprised to see that the cage was full of tinsel and shredded newspaper. She was sure she had put it away clean and empty a few weeks ago. She unclipped the wire mesh that covered the cage and prepared to tip the contents into the bin when the tinsel heaved a great sigh. Startled, she backed away from the cage and reached for a metre stick. Gently she pushed the tinsel aside with the end of the stick, to reveal a small hairy face with floppy ears and long whiskers. The animal's fur was filthy, and it smelt terrible, but it looked up at her with such sleepy, doleful eyes that her heart melted. She snapped the cage back together, grabbed her bag and headed for the car park.

The ofsted was so sleepy that he did not really wake when Miss Hazel lowered him into a bowl of warm, soapy water. The feeling of his skin being massaged was relaxing and so he did not object when the strangely yellow dirty water was tipped away and he was rinsed a second and a third time. He enjoyed being wrapped in a towel and laid on a sunny patch of grass to dry. Miss Hazel carefully cleaned the sink and removed her washing-up gloves. She had no idea what the animal was, but it looked like a long-nosed, ancient guinea pig.

"Whirly-pog," she murmured. "That's the name for you."

The weeks passed and the ofsted's fur became thick and glossy as he enjoyed the diet of fresh grass and rabbit food. His skin tingled in the sunlight and he felt his energy returning. Now that the dust mites in his fur had been washed down the sink, he finally recovered from an extremely long Dose of the Yawns. He still thought back to the forests of his youth with nostalgia but was very content to spend his remaining days foraging with several friendly rabbits in Miss Hazel's garden.

As Zack matured, he grew tall and self-assured. He was known for his quick wit and ready smile. While reading and writing were never going to be his favourite occupation, with practice, support and the help of technology, he conquered The Kraken. He found that he was able to record his ideas effectively using a laptop, and his frustrations melted away. He developed a particular interest in chemistry, and his parents were delighted when he trained to be a doctor.

For many years he kept a small plastic bag of dirty yellow powder stored in his cupboard. Whenever possible, he took it to the medical lab where he performed endless experiments on specks of yellow dust. Within a few years, he had developed a remarkable new sleeping pill. It was ideal for patients recovering from painful illnesses, as it allowed them to wake in good health after many weeks when their pain had passed. In tiny quantities, it also helped people who were distressed, by allowing them a good night's sleep before they woke feeling relaxed and in control. Not long after being licensed, Zack's pills were in huge demand in every hospital in the country.

Zack and Ben remained close friends over the years. Shortly after the new drug had been released, they were relaxing together one Saturday afternoon when a keen, fresh-faced reporter knocked at the door, asking for an interview with the now-famous young doctor.

"Dr Snodgrass, can you explain how you discovered the amazing chemical in your new pill?" asked the reporter eagerly.

Before he answered Zack glanced across at Ben, who winked and grinned.

"Well, like many scientific discoveries, it happened partly by accident, but I did have some help from three slugs and a traffic warden."

"Three slugs and a traffic warden! How on earth did they help to develop a new chemical?"

Zack chuckled.

"I'm afraid, sir, that will remain my secret – forever."

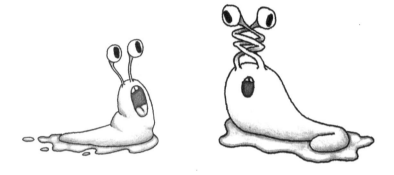